TYLER MORRIS

Manipulation Techniques

The Simple Guide To Understand The Different Techniques To Manipulate People With Dark Psychology

Copyright © 2021 Tyler Morris

All rights reserved.

© **Copyright 2021 - All rights reserved.**

The content contained within this book may not be reproduced, duplicated or transmitted without direct written permission from the author or the publisher.

Under no circumstances will any blame or legal responsibility be held against the publisher, or author, for any damages, reparation, or monetary loss due to the information contained within this book. Either directly or indirectly.

Legal Notice:

This book is copyright protected. This book is only for personal use. You cannot amend, distribute, sell, use, quote or paraphrase any part, or the content within this book, without the consent of the author or publisher.

Disclaimer Notice:

Please note the information contained within this document is for educational and entertainment purposes only. All effort has been executed to present accurate, up to date, and reliable, complete information. No warranties of any kind are declared or implied. Readers acknowledge that the author is not engaging in the rendering of legal, financial, medical or professional advice. The content within this book has been derived from various sources. Please consult a licensed professional before attempting any techniques outlined in this book.

By reading this document, the reader agrees that under no circumstances is the author responsible for any losses, direct or indirect, which are incurred as a result of the use of information contained within this document, including, but not limited to, — errors, omissions, or inaccuracies.

Table of Content

Introduction 4

Chapter 1. Dark Persuasion To Lookout For 10

Chapter 2. Subliminal Persuasion 16

Chapter 3. Psychological Manipulation 21

Chapter 4. Psychological Manipulation Technique 26

Chapter 5. Covert Emotional Manipulation 33

Chapter 6. Covert Emotional Manipulation Tactics 40

Chapter 7. Brainwashing 43

Chapter 8. Brainwashing Technique 47

Chapter 9. Hypnosis 52

Chapter 10. Hypnosis Techniques 59

Conclusion 66

Introduction

Whenever folks try to provide meaning to the notion of demeanor, their responses always come in various forms. Even though some could put their thoughts on the ads and advertisements which are everywhere in contemporary society, advocating you to patronize a specific product or service over the other others' heads fall back into the politicians who attempt to modify the minds of Republicans simply to get yet another vote in the polls. Both instances are right since they are messages targeted at altering the understanding of this topic. The purpose of diversion between ordinary persuasion and dim persuasion is the dark persuasion doesn't necessarily have a moral rationale.

Even though a standard persuader might attempt to convince someone for this individual's own great, a dim persuader does so together with motives that are not always great for another individual. They try to obtain a total grasp of the individual they would like to convince and take pains to do this since they understand the greatest motivation.

While persuasion consistently has ethical consequences, a dim persuader doesn't concern themselves with those consequences. In reality, they are mindful of these, but decide to put their eyes on their goal (s) rather than persuasion as a mental phenomenon in an individual's regular life. It's either that you're the person attempting to convince someone else or you're being persuaded. What makes the distinction between dark and ordinary is that the motivation for this. In mass media, politics, legal and advertising conclusions, persuasion comes to play all of the time. The results of instructing it in such areas are set utilizing persuasion to determine the topic of influence.

There are a few clear and crucial differences between behavioral and other brain control varieties, like brainwashing and hypnosis. Even though these two demands that the topic should be isolated from modifying their thoughts and individuality, persuasion doesn't require isolation. To be able to reach the target, manipulation is utilized on a single individual. Although persuasion may also be performed on a single topic to make them change their thoughts, there's also a chance of using it on a vast scale to alter the heads of an entire group or a whole society.

Because of this, persuasion is a much better mind control procedure and maybe more harmful since it can alter the minds of lots of people at precisely the same time rather than the head of only one individual at one time. Many people produce the error of believing that they have immunity to the consequences of persuasion because they think that they will always have the ability to observe every sales pitch that comes in their way.

They think they'll always have the ability to use logic to grasp what's happening and find a logical decision for this. As a result of how people aren't ever likely to fall for whatever they hear, this might be accurate if they utilize logic. It's likewise feasible to steer clear of persuasion since the debate doesn't augur nicely with the individual's beliefs, whatever the strength of this debate. Some individuals understand how to use clear messages to inspire people to market the industry's newest gadgets or goods. This information action is quite delicate, so the topic won't always recognize it; therefore, it's going to be rather difficult for them to continually have the ability to decide the information they will get.

Every time is said, it's extremely probable that you think about it in a terrible light. That is because it is inclined to automatically consider a conman or salesman who's always attempting to make them modify their view, and that will finally push them till this shift is reached. While black persuasion is notable in earnings and conning clinics, also, there are ways that persuasion may be used permanently, such as in diplomatic relationships between global bodies or at public service attempts. The difference only lies in the method by which in which the practice of persuasion is attracted to perform.

Dark Persuasion Methods

When an individual is prepared to modify the head of the topic by devoting them to do anything against their first frame of mind, the persuader will get some nicely laid out methods to help them reach their targets. Every day that passes, the goal will face various kinds of persuasion. Food manufacturers aim to receive their goal to test the recipes that are new or have them adhere to the earlier ones, even while studios may flaunt their most recent blockbuster films about the faces of the aims. In any situation may be whatever merchandise they're promoting, their principal intent is to generate more revenue, and that's the reason they're attempting to convince you. They couldn't care less about how this may affect you, and that is why they need to be quite careful and proficient in the art of subtle persuasion to make sure they don't deceive you off or make you plump.

As there are also lots of different brands attempting to convince you, they need to locate an exceptional approach to impress their perspectives on you. As a result of the effect of info on a vast selection of individuals, the methods used in it's been a topic of research for several decades, dating back to early times. That is because the influence is a really helpful instrument in controlling a large assortment of individuals. Beginning in the early 20th century, the proper analysis of those techniques started to grow. Bear in mind that the objective of attempting to convince people would be to push a compelling debate in an audience and have the positive.

They'll then internalize this information and embrace it as their fresh mindset or even means of life. Because of this, there's a great need to find very prosperous persuasion methods. Three dark persuasion methods are of fantastic value through recent years. We will go over those three:

Create a Need

This is only one of the most profitable methods of obtaining an individual to change their perspective or lifestyle. The individual hoping to convince a goal will create demand or concentrate on a demand that the topic already has. If that is achieved suitably, it's the capacity of enticing a fantastic deal to your goal. This signifies that to become prosperous, the persuader should interest in the demands that are far more significant to the goal.

This could be their requirement to fulfill their fantasies of fostering their self-esteem. It might also function as a desire for love, food, or shelter. This method will work out nicely since there's not anyway the topic isn't likely to require one or more of these items or need of anything at all for that matter. As there's not always, the goal is not likely to get dreams and ambitions. The persuader will probably simply find strategies to produce the sufferer understand how they can easily help the sufferer attain those dreams. The persuader can also tell their goal the goal will probably recognize their visions if they make certain adjustments to their faith or outlook.

As stated by the persuader, doing this will provide the target with a greater prospect of attaining success. For example, a young guy who wishes to get romantic with a woman may inform her that he'll help her boost her grades and eventually make her parents happy by obtaining a. Still, only when she's friends with his or her although this woman may believe she has finally discovered the salvation she desires, the simple truth is that the young guy is not very curious about how she plays in college. Her teenagers are just a lure for obtaining access to sexual activity.

Appealing to Social Needs

Another technique the persuader may utilize is identifying the goal of social demands. Even though this might not yield as many outcomes and the goal's main requirements will, it's still a powerful instrument in the hands of the persuader. Some are naturally attracted to audiences and want to be desired. They always wish for certain things, not because they want them, but because it includes certain prestige, making them feel like they belong to a bigger course. The idea of appealing to your target's societal needs is what's accessible through several TV advertisements where audiences are invited to purchase a product so they won't be "left behind." When they could recognize and allure to the societal needs of their goal, the outcome is that they can achieve a new field of the goal's interest.

Making Use of Loaded Words and Images

When an individual is hoping to convince someone else, they need to be cautious with their selection of words because words could make all of the difference. When there are many means to say something, one way of stating it might be more potent than another. When it's related to persuasion, among the essential things is understanding how to say the ideal thing at the ideal moment. Words are the most effective tools in communicating and understanding the perfect call-to-action phrases.

Dark persuasion is just one of the most effective dim psychology theories, but regrettably, it's always overlooked and suppressed. This might be because, unlike many different head control procedures, persuasion renders the goal using a selection. At another mind control procedure, the aim is forced to enter.

Occasionally, this is achieved by placing them into isolation to ensure, in conclusion, they don't have any say in the procedure results. Regarding persuasion, the chips have been laid bare (though with the ulterior purpose in dim persuasion), so the goal is made to make the choice they think will fit them best.

Chapter 1. Dark Persuasion To Lookout For

After looking at the different types of persuasion and what they all mean, you may see why dark persuasion is such a bad thing and can be harmful to the victim. Recognizing the different techniques that the manipulator may use can make it easier to understand when used on you.

So, how exactly is a dark persuader able to use this idea to carry out their wishes? There are a few different types of tactics that a dark manipulator is going to use. Still, some of the most common options include:

The Long Con

The first method that we are going to look at is the Long Con. This method is kind of slow and drawn out, but it can be effective because it takes so long, and it is hard to recognize or pinpoint when something went wrong. One of the main reasons that some people can resist persuasion is that they feel that they are being pressured by the other person, making them back off. If they feel that there is a lack of rapport or trust with the person trying to persuade them, they will steer clear. The Long Con is effective because they can overcome these main problems and give the persuader precisely what they want.

The Long Con will involve the dark persuader to take their time, working to earn their victim's trust. They will take some time to befriend the victim and make sure that their victims trust and like them. The persuader will achieve this with artificial rapport building, which sometimes seems excessive, and other techniques will help increase the comfort levels between the persuader and their victim.

As soon as the persuader sees that the victim is adequately readied psychologically, the persuader will begin their attempts. They may start with some insincere positive persuasion. The persuader will lead their victim to choose or do some activities that will benefit the persuader. This is going to serve the persuader in two ways. First, the victim starts to become used to persuasion by that persuader. The second is that the victim will start making that mental association between a positive outcome and the persuasion.

The Long Con will take a long period to complete because the persuader doesn't want to make it too obvious what they are doing. An example of this is a victim who is a recently widowed lady who is vulnerable because of her age and from their grief. After her loss, a man starts to befriend her. This man may be someone she knows from church or even a relative. He starts to spend more time with her, showing immense kindness and patience, and it doesn't take too long for her guard to drop when he comes around.

Then this man starts to carry out some smaller acts of positive persuasion that we talked about before. He may advise her of a better bank account to use or a better way to reduce any monthly bills. The victim will appreciate these efforts and the fact that the man is trying to help her, and she takes the advice.

Over some time, the man then tries to use some dark persuasion. He may try to persuade her to let him invest some of her money. She obliges because of the positive persuasion that was used in the past. Of course, the man is going to work to take everything he can get from her. If the manipulator is skilled enough, she may feel that he actually tried to help her, but the money is lost because he just ran into some bad luck with the investment. This is how far dark persuasion can go.

Graduality

Often when we hear about acts of dark persuasion, it seems impossible and unbelievable. They fail to realize that this dark persuasion isn't ever going to be a big or a sudden request that comes out of nowhere. Dark persuasion is more like a staircase. The dark persuader will never ask the victim to do something big and dramatic the first time they meet. Instead, they will have the victim take one step at a time.

When the manipulator has the target only go one step at a time, the whole process seems like less of a big deal. Before the victim knows it, they have already gone a long way down, and the persuader isn't likely to let them leave or come back up again.

Let's take an example of how this process is going to look in real life. Let's say that there is a criminal who wanted to make it so that someone else committed the crimes for them. Gang bosses, cult leaders, and even Charles Manson did this same thing.

This criminal wouldn't dream of beginning the process by asking their victim to murder for them. This would send out a red flag, and no one in their right minds would willingly go out and kill for someone they barely know. Instead, the criminal would start by having the victim do something small, like a petty crime, or simply hiding a weapon for them. Something that isn't that big of a deal for the victim, at least in comparison.

Over time, the acts that the manipulator can persuade their victim to do will become more severe. And since they did the smaller crimes, the persuader now has the unseen leverage of holding some of those smaller misdeeds over the victim, kind of like for blackmail. Before the victim knows it, they are going to feel like they are in too deep. They will then be persuaded to carry out some of the most shocking crimes. And often, by this point, they will do it because they feel like they have no other choice.

Dark persuaders will be experts at using this graduality to help increase the severity of their persuasion over time. They know that no victim would be willing to jump the canyon or do the big crime or misdeed right away. So, the persuader works to build a bridge to get there. By the time the victim sees how far they are, it is too late to turn back.

Masking the True Intentions

There are different methods that a persuader can use dark psychology to get the things that they want. Disguising their true desires is very important for them to be successful. The best persuaders can use this approach in various ways. Still, the method they choose is often going to depend on the victim and the situation.

One principle used by a persuader is that many people will have a difficult time refusing two requests when they happen in a row. Let's say that the persuader wants to get $200 from the victim, but they do not intend to repay the money. The persuader may begin by saying that they need a loan for the amount of $1000. They may go into some details about the consequences to themselves if the persuader doesn't come up with that kind of money sometime soon.

The victim may feel guilt or compassion for the persuader, and they want to help. But $1000 is a lot of money, more than the victim can lend. From here, the persuader is going to lessen their request from $1000 down to $200, the amount that they wanted from the beginning. Of course, there is some emotional reason for needing the money. The victim feels like it is impossible to refuse this second request. They want to help out the persuader, and they feel bad for not giving in to the initial request when they were asked. In the end, the persuader gets the $200 they originally wanted, and the victim is not going to know what has taken place.

Another type of technique that the persuader can use is known as reverse psychology. This can also help to mask true intentions during the persuasion. Some people have a personality that is known as a boomerang. This means that they will refuse to go in the direction they are thrown away and instead will veer off into different directions.

If the persuader knows someone more of a boomerang type, they can identify a key weakness. For example, let's say that a persuader has a friend attempting to win over some girl they like. The persuader knows that the friend will use and then hurt that girl. The girl is currently torn between a malicious friend and an innocent third party. The persuader may try to steer the girl in the direction of the guy who is a good choice, knowing that she will go against this and end up going with the harmful friend.

Leading Questions

Another method of dark persuasion that can be used is known as leading questions. If you have ever had an encounter with a skilled salesman, verbal persuasion can be really impactful when deployed in careful and calibrated ways. One of the most powerful techniques that can be used verbally is leading questions.

These leading questions will be any questions intended to trigger a specific response out of the victim. The persuader may ask the target something like, "how bad do you think those people are?" This question will imply that the people the persuader is asking about are bad to some extent. They could have chosen to ask a non-leading question, such as "how do you feel about those people?"

Dark persuaders are masters at using leading questions in a way that is hard to catch. If the victim ever begins to feel that they are being led, they will resist, and it is hard to lead them or persuade them. If a persuader ever senses that their victim starts to catch what is happening, they will quit using that one and switch over to another. They may come back to that tactic, but only when the victim has quieted down a bit and is more influenceable again.

The Law of State Transference

The state is a concept that will take a look at the general mood someone is in. If someone is aligned with their deeds, words, and thoughts, this is an example of a healthy and harmonious state. The law of state transference will involve the concept of someone who holds the balance of power in a situation and can then transfer their emotional state onto the other person they interact with. This can be a potent tool for the dark persuader to use against their victim.

Initially, the influencer will force their state to match the state that their target naturally has. If the target is sad and talks slowly, the influencer will make their state follow this format. The point of this is to create a deep rapport with the target.

After we get to this state match, the influencer will alter their state subtly and see if they have some compliance for the victim. Perhaps they will choose to speed up their voice to see if the victim will speed up as well. Once the victim starts to show these signs of compliance, the influencer is at the hook point.

Chapter 2. Subliminal Persuasion

Subliminal persuasion means an advertising message displayed below the threshold of awareness or consumer awareness to persuade or help people change their minds without making them aware of what is going on. This is about affecting individuals with more than words. Some subliminal persuasion methods impact our stimuli with smell, eyesight, sound, touch, and taste.

There are 3 subliminal methods of persuasion that affect everyone. They are:

Building a Relationship

Building a relationship makes the other person feel comfortable. This will open up the individual even more. This can be accomplished through a healthy observation that matches their mood or state. This helps create confidence.

Power of Discussion

The power of discussion and convincing a person is connected to an advertiser's conversion. The correct words and inflections help you to be openly straightforward.

Suggestive Power

Associating useful and desirable stuff in a discussion or interaction enables an individual to become more open to fresh thoughts.

Suggestion and Emotional Intelligence

This stage may be described as having one central and dominant idea focused on the participant's conscious mind, which was to stimulate or decrease the various regions' physiological performance within the participant's body. Using different nonverbal and verbal suggestions was increasingly emphasized to convince the participant easily.

Achieve Optimal Persuasion With Subliminal Psychology

When you can expertly utilize a person's subconscious depths, your control over them is easy and vast. Subliminal psychology is one of the most effective ways to do this. This is an advanced technique, so do not expect to become effective overnight, but know that with time and dedication, you will be able to start putting subliminal messages into the minds of those around you. Once you can do this, you will control what they think and the actions they take. Essentially, you become almost like a puppet master for those around you.

Subliminal Message Techniques

This type of message or affirmation presented either visually or auditory sent in a way below what is considered normal for human visual or auditory perception. For example, a record might be playing on repeat, but you cannot hear it with your conscious mind. However, deep in your subconscious, you hear it and fully register everything that it is saying. In most cases, the messages used are meant to control you in some way or suggest that you do something.

For example, subliminal messages are commonly used in today's world to promote smoking cessation or weight loss. In general, you listen to recorded tapes with a specific message when you are sleeping. Your unconscious mind gets the message, but you never really hear it as your conscious self. Either way, research shows that it can be an effective tool to change your smoking or eating behaviors. You can use a similar technique to help change how people think to make them more vulnerable to the types of persuasion you prefer to use.

This is an effective way to control both your mind and others' minds, but it can be obvious when you do not use the techniques properly. As you read into the primary techniques, pay close attention to how you might introduce a person to them. This is important. Ultimately, your relationship with the person you are seeking to control will determine which of these techniques works the best.

Subliminal Messages During Sleep

This is one of the most common ways to use these types of messages. Most people will use them for themselves in this manner, but you can also use them with people you live with. For example, once you know your spouse is asleep, play a subliminal recording for about one hour. This is all it takes to get your message across.

Now, you must know for sure that they are sleeping, or else you could do more harm than good to your persuasion efforts. When you create your recording, use a calm and steady voice. State precisely what you want the person to do. Use no filler words. Use a maximum of 10 words and simply repeat it for an hour. Then, once the person is sleeping, play the recording at a very low volume close to their head so that their unconscious mind hears it.

Subliminal Flashes

These do not take as long as they are not as risky as the above method. These are a type of visual subliminal message. You can create the flashes to say what you want. What is nice about this technique is that the messages flash so quickly that the conscious mind often does not see what it says. Only the subconscious can understand and record it. So, you can get some control over a person's mind without them knowing what you are attempting to control.

Unless the person you want to do this with knows about subliminal psychology, you can just tell them you want to show them something you created. It is best to do this on a computer so that the screen is large enough to read and keep their full attention during the flashes.

Mixed Subliminal Messages

You can insert subliminal messages into the music or audiobooks that someone listens to regularly. Some programs can do this, so you do not have to be a tech expert to take advantage of this method. Just like with the subliminal messages during sleep, you will use a calm and steady voice. You want the messages to mix into the audiobook or music without being detected. Remember, the subconscious mind will pick up on it even when they cannot hear it when they are awake.

Just make sure to use these messages in something they listen to daily, or almost daily. They must hear it regularly to gain the most control.

Subliminal Notes

This is the easiest method, but it is also the simplest to figure out if you are not careful. You can put messages inside messages throughout your home. For example, when you create the grocery list, add something else you want but do not usually shop for. This puts the thought in the person's head when they are reading the list. This is ideal for smaller things that you want to persuade someone to think or do. So, keep it simple and use this method periodically. Unlike the above methods, it is not a good idea to use it every day.

Chapter 3. Psychological Manipulation

Today, the greatest battles are not fought on battlefields but in our minds and hearts!

And one of the biggest and strongest reasons for an inner battle is psychological manipulation. The biggest problem with psychological manipulation is not only the fact that we are often not prepared to deal with it but also the way we respond to it. And then, our greatest enemy, beyond the manipulator/oppressor, will become ourselves!

One of the main characteristics of psychological manipulation is that the manipulator (who can be a father, a mother, a brother or sister, a romantic partner, or a friend) exercises great control and power over us. And in that instant, our life becomes a real hell, and we live in tremendous anguish.

However, it is crucial to know that we are not, and should not be, impotent in this situation. There are various ways of combating these techniques of psychological manipulation.

The first step is to achieve consciousness, that is, to become aware of these techniques. Take a closer look and learn more objectively how your handlers "work" so you can protect yourself in the future. There are several Manipulation Techniques. See some of them below:

Psychological Manipulation Technique 1: Emotional Blackmail

Emotional blackmail is one of the oldest and most used manipulation techniques employed by human beings. But how does this work exactly?

Many people succumb to this trick because they feel they have no choice. At this point, phrases such as "If you cared about me, you would do this for me" are very common and make the manipulated person feel "forced" to make decisions they do not want. The target will make them anyway just to please the person who manipulates.

To avoid this manipulation technique, you will have to develop a strong sense of yourself, which involves knowing who you are, what your responsibilities are towards others, and who your true friends are. Usually, manipulative and blackmailing people tend to stay away from people with strong and solid personalities. Always remember: you always have a choice, and it is you who decides what you do with your life and how you want to react to the world.

Psychological Manipulation Technique 2: Focus on Negative Aspects

Some people like to put a "brake" on another's ideas and brilliant projects by emphasizing everything that could go wrong with them. These people often push him to doubt his projects and all the good things they would bring if they were put into practice. And at these times, the manipulators offer an endless list of questions that will only serve to create and raise doubts in their target's mind and heart.

For example, if you tell someone, you are thinking of traveling somewhere for a month to relax or go on vacation. If that person does not feel comfortable with the idea for some reason, they will probably react to your news by talking about the big travel hazards and the endless number of negative things that can be expected at the airport, etc.

At such times, if there is no apparent reason for such a reaction from the other person. If you are comfortable with your decision, bearing in mind that it will not harm you or others, choose not to listen to them and follow through with what you have decided.

Do not be overly swayed by this negative thinking pattern. If we think about something a lot, we attract it. If you put it in your head that something bad will happen and focus on it excessively, it is very likely to happen because the thought has life and is a great magnet.

Psychological Manipulation Technique 3: Teenage Rebellion

Unfortunately, sometimes the manipulative person adopts a childlike attitude to respond to his decision or something you have said to him.

For example, you want to leave your home and live independently. At first, it may even seem like everyone is happy and comfortable with your decision. But with time, as soon as you start looking for the perfect apartment, things start happening one after another. Some personal crisis occurs in the family, your mother or father suddenly (re)starts smoking, etc. These are adult people, but they adopt the behavior of a teenager and rebel against the idea.

The easiest way to deal with this is to make them see that their efforts to make you give up are worthless and that you will go ahead with your decision.

At first, it can be challenging and hard for you, especially if you have been exposed to this type of psychological manipulation for a long time. But as time goes by, it will become much easier, and you will see that even the people who manipulate you will come to respect you much more.

Psychological manipulation can be done throughout life, but always remember that you have the power to break this vicious cycle, and above all, remember that only one person can change your life: You!

Love and life together can be sources of well-being, pleasure, and support or a dead-end in which you feel suffocated and as if you are in the dark. The worst is that in many cases, these can be combined in a single day. Both feelings and problems begin when the relationship shifts rapidly. You find yourself immersed in a constant storm of feelings. This mainly happens to those who do not know how to escape such situations.

Many people are immersed in insane and toxic relationships in which they suffer psychological abuse of various kinds. They receive continuous damage to their integrity and honor and levels of disrespect that seem crazy when seen or heard from outside. Still, to the person who is now accustomed to suffering, they do not even produce a minimal reaction in their daily lives.

Love is not an excuse to hide the emotional pain that another person can cause us. It is our responsibility to ourselves to learn how to defend our rights and enforce them. Beyond your insecurity, the parental patterns that you picked up in your childhood, and all the mechanisms of self-deception that you can activate so as not to see reality, at the bottom of your being, you know how to differentiate what is right and what hurts you. That said, sometimes we need someone to tell us in a neutral and unbiased way that we have the right not to put up with what we know we do not deserve. Present a list of the main techniques of manipulation in unhealthy couples.

Manipulation to maintain social control: This technique usually begins in a very subtle way. The couple criticizes friends, family, work colleagues, and anyone in your social circle until they can completely annul the other's social network in such a way that the only source of effort and social support is the couple. This is manifested through jealousy: "If you love me, you would prefer me over your friends," etc. Emotional blackmail: This mechanism is famous for being used between pairs of individuals. It is also widely used by almost everyone, and you likely know it very well. It is about using phrases to handle guilt and repentance as a tactic to get something or as an impediment so that the other does not do something or does not abandon the manipulator. The manipulative person usually uses phrases like: "If you do that, it means you don't love me," "I do not want you to suffer, I would never do that to you," "I want the best for you, even if you let me destroy my life," "If you let me die," etc.

Chapter 4. Psychological Manipulation Technique

What Are Manipulators Looking For

Deceptive people in general: sociopaths, narcissists, liars, and so-called emotional vampires, and it is more a practical question to consider them than a theoretical one. For this purpose, if you've been victims of them at times, it's easier for you to identify and precede them now.

However, it can be said that deceptive people's aims are very straightforward, instrumental and that they follow a specific pattern. Most of them include:

- **Cancel your willpower**: they're trying to sow suspicions and want to bind you to their safety.

- Destroying your self-esteem: bringing a spoken word into the wheel of all you do or have done. We are not helpful and just want to point out the shortcomings.

- Passive-aggressive revenge: By avoiding you, they threaten you. They neglect you when you need them; it's enough to ask something, to get to stand up and not even speak to you.

- Prevent reality: they enjoy confounding people and creating misunderstandings and discussions. We step back after provoking a debate, loving the rants of others.

-

What Are the Psychological Manipulation Techniques?

Gaslighting

Gaslighting is one of the most subtle methods of deception. "It's never happened," "Imagine you" or " You're kidding?" These are some of the words that they use to manipulate and confuse our perception of reality, making us believe things have changed.

This instills an intense sense of anxiety and uncertainty in the victims, to the point of causing them not to trust in themselves, their memory, their understanding, or their judgment.

Projection

The manipulator transfers the negative characteristics to another person or shifts blame for his actions. This is being used heavily by narcissists and psychopaths, saying that the wickedness surrounding them is not their fault but anyone else's.

Meaningless Conversations

The conversation lasts ten minutes. Now is the time for you to leave the conversation. Manipulators say ridiculous things, offer illogical excuses, refer to past events, and throw smoke in the eyes...

We generate discord and misunderstanding. We are doing monologues, and they are trying to confuse you with their gab. Some advice? Get straight to the point and then better if you can leave after 5 minutes. Your feelings would be thankful.

Generalizations and Denigrations

They make generic, vague, and abstract statements. They may seem intellectual. In reality, they are just elusive. Their conclusions are too general; their goal is to demean your e debilitate your opinions.

For example, "you always want to be right," "anything annoys you," "never once you agree." Keep calm. You can opt for irony, with a simple "thank you," or you can ignore them with a curt, "I think you're a little upset. We'll talk later."

Absurdity

Remember that they try to undermine your morals and cause you to question what you believe. They can put words you have never said in your mouth; they will make you think you have the superpower to "read your mind." But that's not the case, and they are just tricks and deceptions. You can help yourself with simulated defeat. Tell them they are right for them to believe it, but stick to your position. You can also respond to their blackmail with an "okay" or with harsh sentences.

The important thing is that you take your self-esteem out of their hands. Remember that they want to demoralize you so that they can control you. After making you weak, the task will be much easier.

Good Mask

"Yes, but..." If you manage to buy a house, they will tell you that it is a pity that you do not yet have a place by the sea; if you are dressed more elegant than ever, they will tell you that another pair of earrings would have been better for you. If you have written an impeccable report, they will tell you that the staple is not well fixed.

But don't let yourselves be influenced: you know what you are worth! Your successes and virtues are worth more than their manipulation techniques. Don't give them any credibility and hang out with people who spend more time pointing out the positives and encouraging you; those who compliment you when you deserve them and who make constructive, non-destructive criticisms.

Positive Reinforcement

Through positive reinforcement learning, behavioral performance is linked to achieving a good outcome. This does not have to be an entity, not even tangible; in many cases, food, liquids, a smile, a verbal message, or the presence of a friendly emotion are likely to be seen as favorable reinforcement.

A father who congratulates his young daughter if she uses the toilet correctly promotes positive reinforcement learning; the same thing happens when a business offers cash incentives to its most successful workers. When we get a bag of potato chips after placing a coin into a retailer.

The definition of "positive reinforcement" refers to the reward that accompanies the action. In contrast, positive reinforcement is the process that creates the connection the learner produces. Nevertheless, the words "reinforcement" and "reinforcement" are frequently used interchangeably, possibly because such a distinction does not exist in English.

From a technical point of view, we can conclude a favorable variance between a particular response and an appetizing stimulus in positive reinforcement. The knowledge of this risk motivates the subject to act to get the reward (or strengthening).

Negative Reinforcement

In comparison to what occurs in the positive, the instrumental response in the negative reinforcement includes the absence of an aversive stimulus, i.e., an event or condition that motivates the subject to avoid or attempt not to come into contact with it.

In behavioral terms, the reinforcement of this technique is the absence or non-appearance of the aversive stimulus. As we stated earlier, the word "negative" refers to the fact that the reward does not consist of obtaining inspiration but in the absence thereof.

This type of learning is divided into two processes: training to escape and train to prevent it. The conduct precludes the presence of the aversive stimulus in the negative reinforcement of avoidance. For example, when an agoraphobic individual avoids using public transport to escape the fear this presupposes, it is reinforced negatively.

On the contrary, the escape is the disappearance of an aversive stimulus present before the subject executes the behavior. Some examples of negative escape reinforcement include an alarm clock that stops by pressing a button, a mother buying a request for her child to stop weeping, or taking a pain reliever to relieve pain.

Brainwashing

The concept of brainwashing is very close to that of 'mind control.' It is an idea without a strictly scientific basis that suggests that the will, thoughts, and other mental facts of individuals can be modified through techniques of persuasion that would introduce unwanted ideas into the psyche of the 'victim.' If we define the concept in this way, we see that it has a marked similarity. However, the term "suggest" is less ambitious.

Although the idea of brainwashing is not entirely wrong, this popular concept has some scientific connotations which have led many experts to reject it in favor of more modest ones. The instrumental use of the term in legal proceedings has contributed to this, particularly in child custody disputes.

Mind control is also known as brainwashing, coercive persuasion, mind control, and mental manipulation. All these terms mean a process that a group or individual systematically uses to force someone to do what they want through thinking of that person. In the majority of cases, these systematic processes are realized without the conscious knowledge of the person.

There are times when we can use mind control over ourselves for a variety of reasons. Self-hypnosis is in this category. We use this kind of mind control, which is voluntary on our part, with our conscious consent, to reinforce a positive idea or to change our minds.

However, this is not the same as the "mind control" phase, or it involves brainwashing. These phrases mean that a person's mind is systematically changed without knowing it, either in the agreement or against his will.

They are carried out through unethical, manipulative tactics, and other means, all designed to control someone's mind. In such cases, they are realized so that one person or group can take full control of others' thoughts and actions. So, when the terms "mind control" and "brainwashing" are used, it is said that specific tactics are used to take control of another at the expense of the manipulated person.

This is interesting because the idea of brainwashing falls under the category of social influence. This is because the concept of brainwashing is used to induce a victim's mental manipulation. This means that brainwashing and mind control are used to completely change how someone thinks and perceives things concerning their beliefs in a particular social device. This is achieved by using various means to change a person's attitudes, behaviors, and thoughts. The person is like a puppet who does everything the manipulator wants.

Chapter 5. Covert Emotional Manipulation

Covert emotional manipulation is used by people who want to gain power or control over you by deploying deceptive and underhanded tactics. Such people want to change the way you think and behave without realizing what they are doing. In other words, they use techniques that can alter your perceptions in such a way that you think that you are doing it out of your own free will. Covert emotional manipulation is "covert" because it works without you being consciously aware of that fact. People who are good at deploying such techniques can get you to do their bidding without your knowledge; they can hold you "psychologically captive."

When skilled manipulators set their sights on you, they can get you to grant them power over your emotional well-being and even your self-worth. They will put you under their spell without you even realizing it. They will win your trust, and you will start attaching value to what they think of you. Once you have let them into your life, they will then begin to chipping away at your very identity in a systematic way. As time goes by, you will lose your self-esteem and turn into whatever they want you to be.

Covert emotional manipulation is more common than you might think. Since it's subtle, people are rarely aware that it's happening to them, and in some cases, they may never even notice. Only keen outside observers may be able to tell when this form of manipulation is going on.

You might know someone who used to be fun and festive. She got into a relationship with someone else, and a few years down the line, she seems to have a completely different personality. If it's an old friend, you might not even recognize the person she has become. That is how powerful covert emotional manipulation can be. It can completely overhaul someone's personality without them even realizing it. The manipulator will chip away at you little by little. You will accept minute changes that fly under the radar until the old a different version of you replaces you, build to be subservient to the manipulator.

Covert emotional manipulation works like a slow-moving coup. It requires you to make small progressive concessions to the person that is trying to manipulate you. In other words, you let go of tiny aspects of your identity to accommodate the manipulative person, so it never registers in your mind that there is something bigger at play.

When the manipulative person pushes you to change in small ways, you will comply because you don't want to "sweat the small stuff." However, there is a domino effect that occurs as you start conceding to the manipulative person. You will be more comfortable making subsequent concessions, and your personality will be erased and replaced in a cumulative progression.

Covert emotional manipulation occurs to some extent in all social dynamics. Let's look at how it plays out in romantic relationships, in friendships, and at work.

Emotional Manipulation in Relationships

There is a lot of emotional manipulation in romantic relationships, and it's not always malicious. For example, women try to modify men's behavior to make them more "housebroken";

that is just normal. However, certain instances of manipulation where the person's intention is malicious, and he/she is motivated by a need to control or dominate over the other person.

Positive reinforcement is perhaps the most used covert manipulation technique in romantic relationships. Your partner can get you to do what he wants by praising you, flattering you, giving you attention, offering your gifts, and acting affectionately.

Even the seemingly nice things in relationships can turn out to be covert manipulation tools and props. For instance, your girlfriend could use intense sex as a weapon to reinforce a certain kind of behavior in you. Similarly, men can use charm, appreciation, or gifts to reinforce certain behaviors in the women they are dating.

Some sophisticated manipulators use what psychologists call "intermittent positive reinforcement" to gain control over their partners. The way it works is that the perpetrator will shower the victim with intense positive reinforcement for a certain period, then switch to just giving her normal levels of attention and appreciations. After a random interval of time, he will again go back to the intense positive reinforcement. When the victim gets used to the special treatment, it's taken away. When she gets used to standard therapy, the special treatment is brought back, and it all seems arbitrary. Now, the victim will get to a place where she becomes "addicted" to the special treatment. Still, she has no idea how to get it. Hence, she starts doing whatever the perpetrator wants, hoping that one of the things she does will bring back the intense positive reinforcement. In other words, she effectively becomes subservient to the perpetrator.

Negative reinforcement techniques are also used in relationships to manipulate others covertly. For example, partners can withhold sex to compelling the other person to modify their behavior in a specific way. People also use techniques such as the silent treatment and withholding of love and affection.

Some malicious people can create a false sense of intimacy by pretending to open up to you. They could share personal stories and talk about their hopes and fears. When they do this, they create the impression that they trust you, but their intention may be to get you to feel a sense of obligation towards them.

Manipulators also use well-calculated insinuations to get you to react in a certain way at the moment to modify your behavior in the long run. Such insinuations can be made through words or even actions. In colloquial terms, we call this "dropping a hint." People in relationships are always trying to figure out what the other person wants out of that relationship, so a manipulative person can drop hints to get you to do what they want without ever having to take responsibility for the actions that you take because they can always argue that you misinterpreted what they meant.

Dropping hints isn't always malicious (for example, if your girlfriend wants you to propose, she may leave bridal magazines out on the table). However, malicious insinuations can be very hurtful, and they can chip away at your self-esteem. Your partner can make insinuations to suggest you are gaining weight. You aren't making enough money or implying that your cooking skills aren't any good. People use hints to get away with "saying without saying," any number of hurtful things that could affect your self-esteem.

Emotional Manipulations in Friendships

Covert emotional manipulation is quite common in friendships and casual relationships. Companies tend to progress slower than romantic relationships, but that just means that it can take a lot more time for you to figure out if your friends are manipulative. Manipulation in friendships can be confusing because even well-meaning friends can come across as malicious. That's because there is a certain social rivalry between even the closest friends, which explains the concept of "frenemies."

Manipulative friends tend to be passive-aggressive. This is where they manipulate you into doing what they want by involving mutual friends rather than directly coming to you. Passive aggression works as a manipulation technique because it denies you a chance of directly addressing whatever issue your friend is raising. So in a manner of speaking, you lose by default.

For example, if a friend wants you to do her a favor, instead of coming out and asking you, she goes to a mutual friend and suggests that she asks you on her behalf. When a mutual friend approaches you, it becomes very difficult for you to turn down the request because of added social pressure. When you say no, your whole social circle now perceives you as selfish.

Passive aggression can also involve the use of silent treatment to get you to comply with a request. Imagine a situation where one of your friends talks to everyone else but you. It's going to be incredibly awkward for you, and everyone will start prying, wondering what the issue is between the two of you, and taking sides on the matter.

Friends can also covertly manipulate you by using subtle insults. They can give you back-handed compliments that have hidden meanings. When you take the time to think about what they meant by the compliment, you will realize that it's an insult in disguise, which will bruise your self-esteem and possibly modify your behavior.

Some friends can manipulate you by going on a "power trip" and controlling your social interactions. For example, there are those friends who insist that every time you hang out, it should be in their apartment or at a social venue of their choosing. Such friends often intend to dominate your friendship, so they are keen to always have the "home ground advantage" over you. They'll try to push you out of your comfort zone just so that you can reveal your weaknesses, and you can then become more emotionally reliant on them.

Manipulative friends tend to excessively capitalize on your friendship, and to a disproportionate degree. They will ask you for lots of favors with no regard for your time or your effort. They are the kinds of friends who will leverage your friendship every time they need something but then make excuses when it's their turn to reciprocate.

Emotional Manipulation at Work

There are many reasons why your colleague may want to manipulate you. It could be you are on the same career path, so he wants to make you look bad. It could be that he is lazy, and he wants to stick you with his responsibilities. It could also be that he is a sadist, and he just wants to see you suffer.

One-way people at work exert their dominance over others is by stressing them out and then, almost immediately, relieving the stress. Say, for example, you make a minor error on a report, and your boss calls you into his office. He makes a big fuss and threatens to fire you, but then towards the end, he switches gears and reassures you that your job is secure as long as you do what he wants. That kind of manipulation works on people because it makes them afraid and gives them a sense of obligation at the same time.

Some colleagues can manipulate you by doing you small favors and then reminding you of those favors every time they want something from you. For instance, if you made an error at work and a colleague covered for you, he may hold it over your head for months or even years to come. He is going to guilt you into feeling indebted to him.

Chapter 6. Covert Emotional Manipulation Tactics

Dark Psychology also spends time looking at Covert Emotional Manipulation. It is more commonly referred to as CEM. CEM is a way to gain real power over someone without them, even realizing it is happening. You will be so enthralled that these sneaky tactics will have you doing things you would not usually agree to.

We have already talked about manipulation, but there are so many different forms of it, which is pretty important. It allows criminals and people with mal intent into your life and breaks you down mentally. The effects of this type of manipulation can last forever if you are not careful. As noted, it is insanely subtle, which means looking for the red flags are very important.

Covert Emotional Manipulation looks different depending on the people involved. Often, the victim will be slowly made to feel like they can't do anything without the other. It is a strange sort of codependency that happens over time. This happens without manipulation on occasion; the difference is when your partner intentionally gets you to behave or think differently.

It may start with offers of help for simple tasks that you usually do on your own. They may follow it up with a critique to make you question your ability to do it. It starts small, but they will continue to poke at it until you start to believe you can't do it on your own truth. You can see it worked into all kinds of things and a ton of relationships.

Depending on who you have allowed doing this to you, it could be mostly harmless. On the other hand, many people with less than genuine intentions could take this to an extreme. This type of manipulation can turn it to flat out brainwashing. In that case, you may lose your free will forever.

People that use CEM against other people pay great attention to detail. This can be endearing as it appears as if they are learning about you. In reality, they are observing your behavior, understanding what makes you tick. This will grant them access to how to manipulate your emotions subtly to get what they want. They are truly hunting for your weaknesses.

The heinous people and criminals that do this in life are calculating. They tend to have bigger plans, and you are simply playing a role. They have no care or regard for how you feel or for the damage they are causing you. All they can see is the outcome that they are striving for. Finding that they are unable ever to sustain relationships is not surprising because of the selfish nature of how they are wired.

As time goes on, CEM turns into something else. What started as little jabs that looked like they were made from love become something much darker. As you start to lose control and bend your will, the aggressor will pounce. They can become domineering. Also, they will begin to tear you down piece by piece to gain complete control.

Playing with someone's emotions is a great way to gain control over them. Some people would rather bombard someone with love to get them to do what they want, rather than being crasser or crude about it. Love bombarding is very typical of the narcissist. It is its form of manipulation, and it can be downright cruel in reality.

You will feel like the most important person in someone's world. You will go along with what they say hook, line, and sinker because you truly trust in what they say. Once this person has you there, they can easily force their will and beliefs onto you. Fighting against this is extremely difficult for some people.

Becoming solid in your belief system will make it more difficult for someone to pray on your emotions. Another way to combat this dark tendency is to work on really knowing yourself. When you spend the time meditating, self-actualizing, and maintaining control of yourself, it is much easier to fend off attacks on your emotions.

When someone manipulates your emotions, it can have a detrimental impact on the rest of your life. Narcissists and Psychopaths cannot often have true feelings. They are shut off, in a way. So, them playing with yours is a simple way to gain control of you and the situation they are in. Practicing NLP's art can also give you signs of when these types of people are trying to harm you.

Gut feelings and red flags should be paid attention to. Naturally, we have instincts, and sometimes something just feels off from the beginning. Maybe you meet someone, and they seem just a little too perfect, or you just feel a bit uncomfortable around them, don't disregard these thoughts and feelings. We are wired to sense danger. This is not just the physical danger that we sense but also an emotional and mental danger. The phrase "go with your gut" is a good one that can help you avoid unpleasant situations.

Chapter 7. Brainwashing

Brainwashing is a particular form of manipulation or control over someone else used through very specific means. Usually, when you use brainwashing, you refer to a particular pattern typically used in hostage situations to try to get the other person to give in to control. Brainwashing most often occurs in the context of trying to get someone else to conform to something new. The purpose of brainwashing comes right down to thought reform—when it is used, the entire purpose is to get compliance and reeducation to encourage someone to become someone they are not. We will also take a look at the most common steps to going through the process.

Defining Brainwashing

Perhaps the first reported source of brainwashing was recorded during the Korean War. During this time, it is said that several American prisoners of war were held in prison camps and were brainwashed into believing that they had engaged in germ warfare and pledged allegiance to communism. When this happened, they were effectively stripped of their identities, forced to comply, and denounced everything that they had known of their past lives. They had their thoughts rewritten through coercion and threat.

Brainwashing is a form of influence designed to be invasive and forceful to break down others' minds. They eventually comply in hopes of protecting themselves from being hurt worse. It becomes self-preservation to do whatever they are told to do to protect themselves. As a result, they are willing to take on complex personas that are entirely dictated by the captors.

The Science of Brainwashing

Brainwashing is believed to work because the agent, that is to say, the person doing the brainwashing, is gaining complete and utter control over the target. This person is being brainwashed in the first place. This makes it so that the agent has complete power over everything and anything related to the individual. The agent gets to determine when needs can be met and how they are. Over time, the result is a systematic destruction of everything that goes into making that person who they are. Over time, because they can't meet their needs, they feel like their identities are destroyed to the point of no longer being viable. Over time, through torture, coercion, and control, brainwashing can occur. Typically, however, it should be noted that the individual's old identity can be returned over time. After leaving the dangerous situation, it is possible, with therapy, for the old identity to be returned.

Using Brainwashing

When brainwashing happens, it is usually done through several steps designed to be as effective as possible. These steps are brutal, but that is the entire purpose of it all. It is designed to be brutal so that it can have its intended effect. Let's go over the steps that go into this method now.

1. Assault on identity: The first step is designed to help to break down the self. It is an assault on your direct identification. It is designed to make you feel like you are not who you are. Typically, in the actual context, the agent will deny everything. They will directly contradict anything that the individual may say is true. As this happens, the individual is repeatedly attacked to the point of exhaustion and eventually even giving in to what the other person said.

2. Guilt: The individual has to be made to feel guilty. This is done so that the individual is more likely to give up his or her identity. When that entire identity is wrapped up in guilt, it is easier to get rid of it and pretend that it is not there than it is to do anything else. By rejecting the identity entirely, the individual is even closer to being brainwashed.

3. Self-betrayal: The stage in which the agent gets the target to agree with what has been said. The agent wants the target to recognize that he or she is bad and that it is time to denounce who they once were. They need to feel like they were wrong to have the opinions that they can do better.

4. Breaking point: That betrayal culminates in what is known as the breaking point—the point at which the individual just cannot cope any longer. At this point, the target goes through what is commonly referred to as a nervous breakdown—sobbing, depression, and generally just not coping well. They may be in the middle of a psychotic episode or may have other problems going on as well. They believe that all hope is lost, and that is the key to the whole process.

5. Leniency: When all seems beyond help, that is when the agent can get in and take control. Usually, with a small kindness—offering a bit of leniency or otherwise offering a drink of water, and that small kindness is enough to make the individual feel indebted.

6. The compulsion to confess: At this point, the target realizes that they have hope. All is not lost, and they can do what it will take to protect themselves. So, what they do is they confess. They want to try to channel and relieve their stress and guilt, so they confess.

7. **Channeling the guilt**: At this point, the target assumes that they are just wrong. The target assumes that they are wrong for some reason, and want to get rid of that sense—which gets connected to their guilt. They wrap all of their guilt about identity together to release it.

8. **Releasing the guilt**: The target realizes the problem is not with him or her, but rather with the guilt and beliefs. They do not have to be permanently bad or problematic—they can get better and do better to release the pain and escape. So, they do this through confessions.

9. **Progress toward harmony:** At this point, the target can begin making a move toward what they perceive as salvation or goodness—they can rebuild themselves to be good. In doing so, in deciding to assimilate and comply, they can make the abuse stop. In denouncing the past, the target can begin choosing the new belief system, making a conscious choice to assimilate and comply. As a result, they conclude that this new identity is reliable and safe, and they follow it.

10. **Final confession**: Finally, the new life is clung to. All old beliefs are rejected, and the individual pledges allegiance to the new life instead.

Chapter 8. Brainwashing Technique

While we are focusing more on the dark psychology that comes with manipulation, you will find examples of manipulation that can occur in our daily lives. Often we don't think that we are doing it at all. We think of manipulation to get what we want from other people, but sometimes we do it to save others' feelings. For instance, how many times have you lied to someone to let them know they looked good in something, even though you didn't think so. You did this to spare their feelings, whether they are a family member or a close friend!

Even though the point of doing this was good, you still were looking to save yourself. You didn't need to be the one who said something means about the other person and how they looked. This kind of manipulation can be seen as a good thing, though, because it was done to spare the other person's feelings in the process.

With that in mind, we will take a brief look at some of the most common manipulation techniques available to us to get what we want. You are sure to recognize at least a few of these as ones that you have used at some point or another in your life, even if you did not think of it as manipulation at the time. Some of the most common manipulation techniques that you can use includes:

Lying is something that we have all done at one point or another. We do this to confuse the other person, make sure that others believe something we want, or even get ourselves out of trouble. You may decide not to go to a party one night because you don't want to go, so you say you had something with family come up. You don't like the gift, but you smile and tell the giver that you love it. We have all used lying at one point or another, and it is considered a type of manipulation. When it comes to a dark manipulator, though, lying will be done in a deliberate way that helps them succeed while ensuring that the other person gets harmed.

Another method that you can use is going to include not telling the whole story. You can imagine yourself as a teenager with this one. Your parents asked you where you were, and you say at the mall with Susan and Sally. But you leave out the fact that the boy they don't like, John, was there as well. You technically were at the mall with your friends, but you leave out the part of the story that will get you in trouble or make someone else mad.

Punishment. This is often reserved for the dark forms of manipulation, but it will still be used on occasion. Without thinking of it as manipulation, we may punish someone else when they don't do what we want. How often have we used the silent treatment against a friend or a spouse who didn't do something that we wanted?

None of us want to end up being the one to blame for something even if we were the ones who did it. We will try to get out of it by denying that anything happened at all. With another tactic known as minimizing, we may admit that something did happen. Still, we will downplay the actions and make it feel like the other person was overreacting and misreading the situation. How many occurrences have we said something we didn't mean. When the person came back to get mad at us about it, we turn it around and minimize it by saying they didn't hear the words the right way. These are probably the two methods of manipulation that we use the most to help keep us out of trouble as much as possible.

Another option that you can work with is going to be known as spinning the truth. This is something that we see all of the time with politicians. It is done so often we can usually see it happening ahead of time. The spinning of the truth will be done to turn some lousy behavior into something that doesn't seem as bad to others. This takes a bit more work to accomplish because you have to think on your feet and develop something plausible. Still, the point is to change up the story to change your perception from other people.

Even though we are not fond of it when other people do this to us, we can all admit that we have played the victim at one point or another. We know that people are more likely to feel bad when we can come up with a sob story. Maybe we try to make one particular person feel bad about how they treated us, and we will do it in front of others so that we can get what we want. Other times we may come up with a big sob story to get out of a group thing, out of late work, and more. The point here is to turn ourselves into a big victim, even though we don't deserve to have that kind of attention or that title.

Positive reinforcement is something that every parent who has wanted to keep their sanity and who has wanted to make sure that their children will follow the rules and behave will use at one point or another. This is where you will reward the behaviors you really like, the behavior you want to make sure sticks around. This can include paying a lot of attention to the target, excessive charm, and expensive presents.

Think of it this way. When your toddler is learning the rules, it is often more efficient to convince them to listen and do what they should when they get a reward. Whether it is a sticker chart, a reward of a toy or some candy or lots of praise, you will find that the more consistent you are with these, the more the toddler will continue to follow the rules. This is precisely how the idea of positive reinforcement is going to work whether you use it on a child or an adult with manipulation.

Diversion can be another way to focus on yourself and work to make sure that the other person doesn't catch on to your true meaning. How many times have you felt that someone was trying to get at your lie or coming close to figuring something you had hidden? Then you would divert the conversation away? No matter how firm they tried to get back to it, you would just push it all back at them or turn the conversation over to a new topic to get the results you wanted and keep the target away from guessing your true intentions.

Sarcasm is a technique that we have all used at one point or another, especially when we want to feel frustrated about something. We may not be able to explain things to someone else. This is going to be done in a way to make us feel more superior to other people and to lower the self-esteem of the victim. Whether we are doing it with friends as a joke or using it against someone else we want to belittle to make ourselves feel better, sarcasm is something that we are all going to be pretty familiar with.

Guilt-tripping is an excellent way for us to make sure that we can get what we want from other people. We will say things like the other person have life easy, really selfish, or don't care about us. This will make the other person feel bad and like something they did was wrong, even if they were trying to help you out with something, and they are more likely to want to try and help you some more.

How many occurrences have we all tried to use some form of flattery to get what we want from other people? This helps us get on the other person's right side, and all it takes is flattering the target praising them and using all our charm. No matter who they are, the target will be happy to get all of this praise and compliments, and it will help lower their guard a little bit in the process. This is a great one that can be used when we want to get a new job or gain up in our position when an opening happens.

As you will notice, there are many different methods of manipulation that we can use in our daily lives. It doesn't seem to matter whether we are using them just to help us get by or if we are trying to use them to help us be dark manipulators and always get what we want, no matter the consequences. How many of the methods on the list have you used at one point or another in your own life to get what you wanted?

Chapter 9. Hypnosis

What is Hypnosis

There have been many definitions of what hypnosis is. The American Psychological Association has defined hypnosis as a cooperative interaction where the hypnotist will give suggestions to the person; he picks which he or she will respond to. Edmonton said that a person is simply but in a deep state of mind when undergoing hypnosis. Hypnosis is, therefore, when a person enters a state of mind in which a person finds himself or herself vulnerable to a hypnotist's suggestions. Hypnosis is not new to us because many people have seen it in movies, cartoons, or been to magic shows or performances where participants are told to do usual acts, and they do it. For sure, some people believe that hypnosis exists and would do anything to avoid being a victim, while others believe that its fiction.

Induction

Induction is considered as stage one of hypnosis. There are three stages in total. Induction aims to intensify the partaker's expectations of what follows after, explaining the role they will be playing, seeking their attention, and any other steps needed during this stage. There are many methods used by hypnotists to induce a participant to hypnosis. One of them is the "Braidism" technique, which requires a hypnotist to follow a few steps. This technique is named after James Braid. The first step would be to find a bright object and hold it in your left hand and specifically between the middle, fore, and thumb fingers.

The object should be placed where the participant will fix their stare and maintain the stare. This position would be above the forehead. It is always crucial that the hypnotist remind the partaker to keep their eyes on the object. If the participant wonders away from the object, the process will not work. The participant should be focused entirely on the item. The participant's eyes will begin to dilate, and the participant will start to have a wavy motion. A hypnotist will know that his participant is in a trance when the participant involuntarily closes his or her eyelids when the middle and forefingers of the right hand are carried from the eyes to the object. When this does not happen, the participant begins again, guiding that their eyes are close when the fingers are used in a similar motion. Therefore, this puts the participant in an altered state of mind. He or she is said to be hypnotized. The induction technique has been considered not to be necessary for every case. Research had shown that this stage is not as important as already known when it came to the induction technique's effects. Over the years, there have been variations in the once original hypnotic induction technique, while others have preferred to use other alternatives. James Braid's innovation of this technique still stands out.

Suggestion

After Induction, this follows the suggestion stage. James Braid left out the word suggestion when he first defined hypnosis. However, he described this stage as attempting to draw the partaker's conscious mind to focus on one central idea. James Braid would start by minimizing the functions of different parts of the partaker's body. He would then emphasize using verbal and non-verbal suggestions to get the partaker into a hypnotic state. Hippolyte Bernheim also shifted from the physical form of the partaker. This well-known hypnotist described hypnosis as the Induction of a particular physical condition, which increases one's susceptibility to the participant's suggestions. Suggestions can be verbal or one that doesn't involve speech. Modern hypnotist uses a different form of suggestions that include non-verbal cues, direct verbal suggestions, metaphors, and insinuations. Non-verbal suggestions that may be used include changing the tone, mental imagery, and physical manipulation. Mental imagery can take two forms. One consists of those that are delivered with permission and those that are done none the less and are more authoritarian.

When discussing hypnosis, it would be wise if one would be able to distinguish between the conscious mind and the unconscious mind. While using suggestions, most hypnosis will try and trigger the conscious mind other than the unconscious mind. In contrast, other hypnotists will view it as a way of communicating with the unconscious mind. Hypnotists such as Hippolyte Bernheim and James Braid, together with other great hypnotists, see it as trying to communicate with the conscious mind. This is what they believed. James Braid even defines hypnosis as the attention that is focused upon the suggestion. The idea that a hypnotist will be able to creep into your unconscious mind and order you around is next to impossible as according to those who belong to Braids school of thought. The determinant of the different conceptions about suggestions has also been the nature of the mind. Hypnotists such as Milton Erickson believe that responses given are normally through the unconscious mind. They used the case of indirect suggestions as an example. Many of the nonverbal suggestions, such as metaphors, will mask the hypnotist's true intentions from the victim's conscious mind. A form of hypnosis that is completely reliant upon the unconscious theory is a subliminal suggestion. Where the unconscious mind is left out in the hypnosis process, then this form of hypnosis would be impossible. The distinction between the two schools of thought is quite easy to decipher. The first school of thought believes that suggestions are directed at the conscious mind will use verbal suggestions.

In contrast, the second school of thought who believe that suggestions are directed at the unconscious mind will use metaphors and stories that mask their true intentions. In general, the participant will still need to draw their attention to an object or idea. This enables the hypnotist to lead the participant in the direction that the hypnotist will need to go into the hypnotic state. Once this stage of suggestion is completed and is successful, the participant will move onto the next stage.

Susceptibility

It has been shown that people are more likely to fall prey to the hypnotist tactics than others will. Therefore, it will be noted that some people can fall into hypnosis easily, and the hypnotist does not have to put so much effort. At the same time, for some, getting into the hypnotic stage may take longer and require the hypnotist to put quite the effort. While for some, even after the continued efforts of the hypnotist, they will not get into the hypnotic state. Research has shown where a person has reached the hypnotic state at some point in their lives. They will likely be susceptible to the hypnotist's suggestions, and those who have not been hypnotized, or it has always been difficult for them to reach that state. It will be likely that they may never be able to get that hypnotic state.

Different models have been established to determine the susceptibility of partakers to hypnosis. Research done by Deirdre Barrett showed that there are two types of subjects that considered being more susceptible to hypnosis and its effects. The two subjects consist of the group of dissociates and fantasizers. Fantasizers can easily block out the stimuli from reality without the specific use of hypnosis. They daydream a lot and also spent their childhood believing in the existence of imaginary friends. Dissociates are persons who have scarred childhoods. They have experienced trauma or child abuse and found ways to put away the past and become numb. If a person belongs to this group finds him or herself daydreaming, it will be associated in terms of being blank and fantasizing. These two groups will have the highest rates of being hypnotized.

Types of Hypnosis

A hypnotist can use different types of hypnosis as a participant. Each of them will use different ways and will help with certain issues. Some types of hypnosis will assist in weight loss, while others will help a participant relax.

Traditional hypnosis

This type of hypnosis is very popular and used by hypnotists. It works by the hypnotist, making suggestions to the participant's unconscious mind. The participant who is likely to be hypnotized by this does what he is told and does not ask many or frequent questions. If one was to self-hypnotize themselves, they would do this by using traditional hypnosis. As we have said, this type of hypnosis is very popular, and this could be attributed to it not requiring much skill, and it is not technical. The hypnotist will just have the right words and just tell the participant what to do. This might pose a problem to the hypnotist where the participant is a critical thinker and can analyze a given situation.

Neuro-Linguistic Programming (NLP)

This type of hypnosis gives the hypnotist wide criteria for the methods they can use in hypnosis. The hypnotist can save time during the process as the hypnotist will just use the same thought patterns to create the problem in the participant. For example, if it is stress, the same thought pattern causing this stress will be used to counter the stress.

NLP Anchoring

To understand how anchoring works, think of a particular scent. The first time you had that scent, you were going through some feeling in which the unconscious mind attached these feelings to that scent. Through this, the scent will become the anchor for those particular feelings. Every time you heard the scent, those feelings come rushing back, triggered by the unconscious mind. This type of NLP has been useful to hypnotists in the process of hypnosis. If you won a prize or some money, for example, the hypnotist will try and recreate those feelings you had when you won the prize. While recreating these feelings, the hypnotist will ensure the participant does an action during this process. Each time the subject does the said action, they will be reminded of those feelings.

This type of NLP can motivate a person to accomplish their goals, for example, if they are trying to be healthier or lose weight. The hypnotist will create a positive anchor that is in line with the mental image of the participant. The mental picture will be that of a sexy slim body. This image will be used as the motivator to start losing weight.

NLP Flash

This technique should only be done by a certified professional because it is considered very powerful and used to alter thoughts and emotions around the participant's unconscious mind. It is deemed to be helpful to persons who experience chronic stress or are addicted to a substance. Here is what the hypnotist will do; he or she is addicted to a substance instead of it, causing some feelings of happiness the act will now cause feelings of pain.

Where the person had chronic stress, the cat will bring a sense of relaxation. Those addicted to substances such as cigarettes and alcohol will now feel pain when they take these substances, which can effectively help them get over their addiction.

Chapter 10. Hypnosis Techniques

Once you have mastered the process of hypnosis that can often be called the long process, you can begin to use another powerful form of hypnosis to your advantage, instant hypnosis. These techniques play with the basics of the mind and what can happen to everyone from time to time daily. Have you ever gazed out of the window and simply watched the rain come down? What about listening to music that makes you feel soothed and relaxed? Maybe watching a favorite movie or television show, and you just feel yourself tune out. Often when this happens, you may not even notice that your brain has checked out. You're comfortable, relaxed, and completely absorbed in what you are doing. It happens every day and has three characteristics that are telltale signs.

1. Increased focus and concentration.

2. Increased relaxation of the body.

3. Increased access to the subconscious mind.

Hypnosis simply uses this natural state of things to put your subject into that state of mind as quickly as possible.

The Handshake Technique

This technique requires that you and the subject have some trust between you. As you will reach out your hand to shake with and then pull sharply towards yourself, you will forcefully, but calming say the word sleep as you do this. If you don't have a little trust built between you, this could just as easily backfire and make the subject tense when you pull them in. How does this technique work so easily? It works by using two different methods of inducing hypnosis: moving the subject off balance, so the brain does not have time to compute a response and giving the forceful suggestion of sleep, which seems like a good idea to the brain. People are far more suggestive than they think, and that is how this simple but powerful instant technique can work.

Falling Backward Method Technique

This form of instant hypnosis again works in the process of putting someone off balance and giving them a suggestion to follow. Instead of pulling them forward towards you, however, the subject will tip slightly backward. By following simple steps, this process can put your subject under in less than a minute:

Step 1: Ask your subject to stand with their feet together and their arms hanging loosely at the side. As they get into a position to explain what you will be doing with them step by step to know what is coming next, you will let them also know this will test their relaxation reflexes.

Step2: Move to stand directly behind your subject and place both hands on their shoulders.

Stand close enough to control them as they fall, but not close enough so that they will fall directly on you. Control the fall but don't take too much weight.

Place one foot in front of the other, and you will be able to keep the right balance to hold their weight as they fall back. Tell the subject this is just a trial run.

Step 3: Ask your subject to relax and explain that you will pull them a few inches back but that you will not let them fall. Place a strong emphasis on this fact that you will not let them fall and ask them to stay relaxed and bend their body at the ankles only, not at the waist, knees, or anywhere else.

Step 4: With your hands still on the subject's shoulders, ask them to close their eyes and pull them back only a few inches. A space of two or three inches is sufficient. Remember not to jar of force them, but allow them to gently tip backward and then rock them forward again. Keep your hands firmly on their shoulders and stand the client upright again, ensuring they regained their balance.

Step 5: If your subject seems relaxed, move on to the next step. If not, assure the subject that they have done well, and repeat the earlier step again to make certain the subject knows what to expect. You may find that certain nervous subjects might require several attempts before they're fully comfortable.

Step 6: After having them fall back, you can sit them down and use a short and brief deepening technique to make sure they are deep in hypnosis. This is usually done simply using phrases such as "move deeper and deeper into hypnosis, relax" repeat this as needed to make sure that your subject is deep into hypnosis.

The Eye Test

To confirm for both you and the subject that a state of hypnosis has been reached with an instant technique, you want to use this simple process. With your subject comfortable and sitting, follow this process:

Step 1: "You feel your eyes are very heavy and completely relaxed. Each muscle around them is now relaxed. This makes your eyelids very heavy."

Step 2: "On the count of three and not before, I will ask you to open your eyes. When I ask this, you will not be able to. You are so completely relaxed that your eyelids are too heavy. You will not be able to open your eyes because your eyelids are so heavy, and you are so relaxed that you will not even try to open them."

Step 3: "Your eyelids are closed. Heavy. Sealed shut, and you can't open them."

Step 4: "One. Your eyes are closed; your eyelids are heavy. You can't open them, not even if you try. You simply can't open them. They are too heavy, so very heavy."

Step 5: "Two. You cannot open your eyes."

Step 6: "Three. Your eyes are tightly closed. Try opening them. You cannot open them, right? Your eyelids are too heavy. Stop trying, just simply relax your eyes again, no more trying to open them. As go your eyes, so you should go your body. Relax."

When you are doing this process, you do not allow your subject to try opening their eyes for more than a second or two. If you give them too much time, they will eventually be able to force their eyes open, and once they have done that, they will come out of hypnosis. If they can open their eyes right away without any effort, they have not been put under, and you will have to start again. If this does occur and open their eyes, simply tell them it's okay and that their eyes were not relaxed enough, so you will begin again. Remember to keep a festive air.

Relaxation Technique

Therapists usually ask you to make yourself feel at home and be comfy during an introduction meeting. They may even provide you with a soft couch to lay on. Why? Are they just being courteous? The truth is, it's more than that. Therapists use relaxation as a common method to induce hypnosis. If you are relaxed, you will likely fall into a trance quicker, and your mind becomes more open to accepting suggestions. Listed are some of the usual methods to promote relaxation:

- Be comfortable.
- Lay down.
- In your head, start to count down.
- Control your breathing.
- Tense your muscles and then relax.
- Speak in a calm, soft tone.

Handshake Technique

The father of hypnotherapy, Milton Erickson, became famous for using a handshake technique to get a person into a hypnotic trance. Handshake is a common greeting, but in hypnosis, it can be more than just a gesture. Hypnotists do not just shake hands in a normal way. They interrupt the subject's mind by grabbing his wrist or pulling him forward to break the balance. Because the pattern established by the subject's mind was interrupted, the client's subconscious mind will suddenly be open to suggestions.

Eyes Cues Technique

The brain has two spheres – the conscious and creative side (right) and the practical and subconscious side (left). When we are in a conversation with someone, we look for feedback to know how they feel or react to what we say. Watch your subject's eyes. Are they looking to the right? Or are they looking to the left? Remember, when they're looking to the right, that suggests that they are conscious of the current situation. If they are looking to the left, that means they are in subconscious thought.

Visualization Technique

You can use visualization to induce your subject into a hypnotic trance and make suggestions. For instance, ask your subject to visualize a room that they know very well. Instruct them to visualize each detail in that room: the windows, the smell, the lighting, the color of the wall, the texture of the floor. Then, ask them to visualize a room they do not know, such as your office. As they struggle to remember the exact details of the room they are less familiar with, they open their minds to suggestions.

Arm Levitation Technique

You can perform this by asking your subject to close their eyes. Then, ask them to notice the difference between their arms. They might say their arms are heavy or light. Subconsciously, they will enter a trance and lift their arms or make their mind believe they have lifted their arms. Either way, induction is a success.

Sudden Shock/Falling Backwards Technique

As with the handshake technique, a subject in shock can enter into a trance. You might have heard about "trust falls." The feeling of falling backward can put the body into shock. Thus, it opens the mind to accept suggestions. Of course, you must catch your subject and be very careful not to drop him/her.

Hypnotic Trigger Technique

There are several forms of hypnotic triggers. A trigger lets the subconscious remember a desired feeling or action that is suggested while under hypnosis. Here are some examples:

- Finger snap
- Clap
- Sound of ball
- Opening eyes
- Standing or sitting

Touch Technique

In this technique, the hypnotist or psychiatrist will put the subject into a relaxed state of mind. Then, gently, the hypnotist will tap the subject's hands with his/her own with slight pressure. With a pen held directly in front of the subject, they will follow it with their eyes while visualizing a perfect place in their mind. This technique needs to be repeated several times during each session. Every after the session I have with this technique, I am always relaxed and feel better.

Conclusion

How to Hypnotize People

Talking about any professional hypnosis instructor, they notify their clients that a successful hypnotherapist is usually confidential. Ideally, you motivate confidence in your clients with the method of 'Personality Assurance.' In other words, the clients get to the state, whereby they feel better when you are around. Of course, this is the same when you invent the method of delivering speeches to hypnotize your audience. To start with, you need to cultivate confidence in your ability when with the audience. You portray a nervous mood at the same time.

Ideally, you tend to put your client/audience in the state. They feel like you cannot find them in the room; you portray the narratives in their minds. This could be done with the ideology of focusing your attention so carefully to ensure that your words have a real effect on their perception, consciously, and unconsciously. Changing the functioning of your immune system or blood circulation tends to be done by a competent hypnotist.

A good narrator must understand the idea of you wanting to be sufficiently convincing your listeners to concentrate on what you say. This is necessary because you need them to disassociate themselves from their concerns and situations to travel to different times, places, and opportunities with you. So, at least for a while, you tend to make them understand the benefits of implementing the new ways of seeing reality.

Helping people learn new ways of responding to life, with the aim of not letting low confidence, phobias, and attention mess them up is so useful for 'Therapy hypnosis.' You concentrate your audience's attention so selectively when you speak with power that they become hypnotic rather than purely aware of the essence of their living. Therefore, this kind of education seems more profound for people.

Avoiding the Boredom Trance

However, it appears that various kinds of trances are in the crowd. You tend to hypnotize the audience by making them be in the state of leaving the room psychologically when you aren't inspiring them. Instead, the groups will try not to obey your concept and try to avoid your voice. In most cases, they begin imagining what they will do for the day, what their next social arrangements will be like, or even what they will cook for lunch. The audience/participant tends to be disassociating, but not in the ways we would like. However, it appears that the specific technique to guide your audience in the proper direction seems to be available.

Crowd Hypnosis

Professional public presenters tend to captivate the audience with thoughts and words. Also, what they will use are the anticipation, vocabulary, narrative, and initial pace. This means that implementing the ideas for their audience to act on in the future will be their ideal objective. This method tends to be very useful when it comes to hypnotizing the audience. This means that the hypnotic speakers don't give just facts. Instead, they serve the audience with an experience that will improve how they feel, think, or even behave.

Prepare Your Speech With Words That Appeal to Feelings

'Nominalization' happens to be the term in which the people who have to travel inwards to communicate with personal meanings are called. This idea helps in hypnotizing the audience. These happen to be words like mighty, lovely, devotion, wisdom, power, and so on. What's just needed is that you ensure that you align the terms with what you mean. Ideally, such correctly used terms need to contain more than mere concrete words, but words evoke feelings.

Paint Vision of Hearing Minds Through Combining Senses

We portray a paradise-like experience to someone, the moment we hypnotize them. And indeed, in pictures, words, sounds, feelings, tastes, and as well as emotions, we dream. You need to tell what you've seen, felt, heard, and tasted when you say a story about something that has happened to you when giving speeches.

Ideally, an address becomes more elegant with the implementations of this sensory appeal. For instance, "When I heard a sickening scream, I was carrying a huge bag through the mall, I turned around and saw two giant guys trying to mug an old lady who pushed them into the realm" sounds more appropriate. Compared to this, "I went to the shopping center and witnessed a serious physical conflict."

Tell All Your Stories to Hypnotize

When there are great stories to tell, tell your viewers/audience overwhelmingly, even at the moment when you're giving a talk about molecular biology.

Fascinate With Your Voice

Think about words that have significance and relevance. So, in other words, you need to speed up with your voice at times. Then sometimes slow down a bit. Perhaps, this shouldn't happen every single time to avoid getting upset. You need to reduce the speed you implement in your words when you make an argument of significance. Then, also, you can even talk to a real hypnotist calmly and on slow delivery, periodically.

Use Suddenness

We tend to go into a hypnotic spell when we're shocked or surprised, not only when we loosen up.

Humor, as it is, tends to amuse someone. So, great speakers implement the idea of using humor because it is hypnotic. There tends to be a punch on a punch line in some other perspectives, and that is because it is surprising. Mainly, the shock is often used by the hypnotists from different stages to track subjects quickly into a hypnotic state.

Be Powerful

You can create a hypnotic state for people by merely exerting power over others. Look at how people are likely to follow a person who appears to be powerful blindly. When you do this, you can get a following, and the people following you will do what you say because they want to please you and stay in your presence.

You can use this technique among your friends, family, coworkers, and any person you have a pre-existing relationship with. You want to exert your power over time so that it does not feel too aggressive. Once you notice you have followers, start small with what you are asking. They will do it without even thinking twice about it. Over time, you can ask for larger things, and you will have no trouble getting them.

Mirroring

Now, the powerful approach works for people, you know, but what about strangers? This is where mirroring comes into play. This allows you to quickly develop a rapport with someone once they see you both have someone in common. This can almost put them into a trance because they will naturally like you and want to please you since they will perceive both of you as very similar.

To successfully use this technique, pay attention to the stranger's common phrases and body language. Look at their behaviors. Exhibit these things back at them. As you continue your interaction with them, it will not take long to notice the similarities. You do not even have to lie about things you have in common. Simply mirroring their language and behaviors is enough to get them under your spell.

Use Stories

The good stories can put people into a trance-like state. Think back to when you were a kid, and your parents would read stories to you before bed. This would induce a deep state of relaxation. The same is true when you are an adult.

As you are talking to people each day, add in some anecdotes. This shows you personally and can even give you a sense of power and authority. You want people to visualize what you are saying, so use imagery to tell your story.

For example, you want a person to move something breakable because you just do not want to risk it. Do not just ask them to move it carefully. State that you do not want the vase to be dropped since it can shatter. They will visualize the vase shattering, forcing them to not only be careful when moving it, but they will volunteer to do it. They will almost see completing the task successfully as a type of personal challenge.

Lengthy Speeches

When you want to induce hypnosis on a large group, lengthy speeches are how to do it. Think about the television evangelists you have seen. They essentially use this form of hypnosis to get people to hand over thousands of dollars every time they hold a service.

When they are delivering their speech, they take a few pauses. They use varied voice tones to annunciate points and keep people completely engrossed in what they are saying. They know what their message is, and they repeat it frequently. However, they often use different phrasing, so no one in the audience ever feels like something is being forced on them.

It is not uncommon for them to tell you exactly what to do without directly telling you to do it. When you're in this type of situation, you are so enamored with the speaker that you will do just about anything they ask. They always present their lengthy speech, and then they just pass the collection basket. They do not ask you to donate because they know you will. After all, you feel dedicated to them.

You can use this technique too. You do not need an auditorium for it either. If you need something from a person or a group of people, plan out a speech. Make sure that those you are talking to feel empowered throughout the lesson. By the time you get to the end, you have already subconsciously implanted in their minds what you want. You will not need to ask for it. You will just get it.

For example, you want people to invest in your new business idea. Give them a speech about the business, about how much starting it would mean to you, and then insert a bit of a sob story about how this is your dream. Still, financially, you cannot swing it. After listening to your dramatic speech, they will feel compelled to invest.

Stacking

This is a hypnotic technique that works because you nearly overwhelm the people you are talking to. With this technique, you essentially bombard people with information. They are learning so many new things that they do not have time to sort through it. They do not feel they need to check facts because you are speaking with such authority that they automatically believe what you are saying. By the time you end your thoughts, you have essentially put them into a trance.

Cold Reading

This is something that psychics use to convince people that they can read their minds and predict their future. You will start by making a vague statement. For example, if you know a person to be shy, you will state this. You know it is accurate, and they will elaborate, giving you further information. You will use this additional information to make other predictions essentially. Once a person feels that you have this almost clairvoyant ability, they are more prone to believe anything you tell them.

www.ingramcontent.com/pod-product-compliance
Lightning Source LLC
Chambersburg PA
CBHW071123030426
42336CB00013BA/2182